BEER

THOMAS LANGE
& JO FORTY

CHARTWELL
BOOKS, INC.

This edition first published in 1998 by
PRC Publishing Ltd,
Kiln House, 210 New Kings Road, London SW6 4NZ

CHARTWELL BOOKS. INC.
A division of BOOK SALES, INC
P.O. BOX 7100
Edison, New Jersey 08818-7100

ISBN 0785 809 295

Printed and bound in China

Acknowledgments

The bulk of the photographs in this book were taken by
Simon Clay; the Author and Publisher should also like to
thank Marston's for providing the photographs on pages
4, 7, and 8, and Einbecker for those on pages 40 and 41.

Thomas Lange is a member of the British Guild of Beer
Writers and is involved in bringing some of finest beers
into the UK through the award-winning company
Brewers Imports. He has extensive brewing contacts in
Continental Europe and frequently organises trips to
breweries.

Introduction

Archaeologists have ascertained that beer was brewed over 5,000 years ago by the early civilizations of Egypt and Sumer—and it is from these peoples that the oldest known recipes derive. However, the very earliest brewing was probably carried out in Neolithic times, when man first began to harvest and store cereals and discovered in turn the fermenting process and how it could be put to use.

Beer was, and still remains, much more than the oldest known alcoholic drink, having been used and consumed in many different ways for many different reasons. It was taken medicinally in the treatment of the sick, religiously in ceremonies and rituals honoring both the gods and the dead, as a form of pay and barter, as well as an important source of nutrition. Significantly both bread and beer use virtually the same ingredients, and their development is intertwined. The ancient Sumerian word for beer in fact meant "liquid bread," as they made their brews by fermenting bread in water.

There was a time before modern refrigeration and bottom fermentation when beer could only be made locally and could only be made for part of the year, because it would neither keep

nor travel well. The monasteries of the Middle Ages, equipped with Roman and Greek manuscripts of Egyptian techniques, became famous for their brews, eventually helping the evolution of beer towards that which we drink today with two major innovations: the replacement of other flavorings with hops and the technique of bottom fermentation.

With the growth of cities and urbanization came specialization and commercial breweries. Beer became an important source of revenue to civil and national authorities alike, with laws enacted to preserve its quality and purity. Though at the beginning of the nineteenth century beer was still top-fermented and short-lived, within a few decades the industry changed dramatically with the advent of bottom fermentation, steam-powered refrigeration and transport, and pasteurization. These changes led to a massive rise in production, as beer could be made all year round and kept longer too, as well as be transported swiftly to areas of increased demand and consumption.

One common misconception is that beer is a specific drink—along with stout, ale, porter, bitter, and lager. In fact beer is a generic term encompassing all these different types—meaning anything brewed with grain (although usually barley), hops and yeast. The main difference between the different types of beer tends to be in the sort of yeast used—whether top or bottom-fermented— although other variations occur in the choice of barley, hops, and water, as well as in the actual brewing techniques of individual brewers. The variations in barleys, yeasts, water, and their ratios and combinations in the brewing process itself,

Below: Delivery the traditional way by Morrell's Brewery.

make the difference between light or dark beers. The country of origin is, of course, important, as is the type of beer being made: yet all beers are fundamentally the same. What makes the vital taste difference—using top or bottom fermenting yeasts—has its effect in the all important stage of fermentation and this is what determines the character of a particular beer.

The lager revolution led by Central European brewers swept aside many of the older beers, except in northern Europe where they seemed to co-exist amicably. The 1970s was the nadir of dark malted ales, victims of omnipresent mass-produced lagers. (Though there were always exceptions, such as the Irish and their Guinness.) Since then the world has witnessed an astonishing revival in local beer production across all the continents, with hundreds of micro-breweries developing and producing their own speciality beers. Though light-colored lager still predominates, there has been a huge increase in interest and demand for all the other older types of beer.

HOW IS BEER MADE?

The main element of beer is water—pure water in constant supply. The great brewing cities, such as Burton, Budweis, Dublin or Dortmund, all benefit from the accessibility and quality of their water. After water, the grain—usually barley— is key to producing the malt from which beer is made.

Barley

Most of the barley which goes for brewing is specifically grown for the purpose. The quality varies according to the climate, and the prevailing weather during the growing season, as well as the location of the barley field. Two-rowed barley is the most traditional for brewing, but six-rowed barley is also used. Barley has always been the favorite grain of choice because of its characteristics—from its high yield of fermentable sugars to its husks, which act as a natural filter.

To brew beer, barley is malted—steeped in water until it begins to germinate—and then dried in a kiln. Every element of the process produces variations: the type of grain, where it was grown, moisture within the grain, the temperature, and for how long. It is at this stage that the color and resonance of the beer is produced. Malting releases the starches that will turn into the sugars vital to the fermenting process when the malt is mixed again with hot water. To this mixture, known as the "wort," hops and—later when the wort has cooled—yeast are added. Both these vital ingredients give bitterness, flavor, and aroma to offset the malt's sweetness, as well as to combat its latent bacteria and act as a natural preservative. Finally the brewer may combine a number of maltings to produce the resultant brew.

Wheat

Some of the most refreshing beers contain a proportion of wheat mixed with the barley. Although wheat has a long history of use in brewing, at different points in the story of beer wheat has almost vanished from the stage, yet it always reappears. Perhaps one reason for its regular lack of popularity among brewers is that it lacks a husk and consequently can easily clog the mashing vessels and other brewery machinery. For this reason it cannot be used exclusively but instead as an adjunct to the barley. Called *Weizenbier* or *Weisse*—wheat or white, partly to describe the contents but also the appearance—wheat beer has a light color and a very thirst-quenching palate. The main center of production of wheat beers is in Southern Germany, though Belgium produces a selection too. From these sources American and Canadian wheat beers derive.

Yeast

As with wine, bread, yogurt and many other drinks and foods, beer depends upon yeast. Yeast is a single-celled micro-organism that is invisible to the naked eye, which consumes the sugars from the malt, converting them into alcohol and giving off carbon dioxide. Needless to say this was not understood when brewing first began, but it still took place due to the prevalence of yeast in the air, in the brewing vessels and on the tools used—everywhere in fact. An old style of fermentation used by commercial brewers is called "lambic," where windows are left open to receive wild yeast from natural airflows. Obviously this method is prone to variance, but brewers noticed that the yeast "foam" on the top of the brew would aid the fermentation of the next batch and began to keep it. This top fermentation was the beginning of yeast development and selection. Bottom-fermenting yeasts were selectively cultured in Germany in the fourteenth century when it was found that, when cold-stored in caves, yeast would sink to the bottom of the containers and also wild yeasts could not impinge on the brew because of the

Above: Weighing hops.

temperature. However it was not until the invention of the microscope and pasteurization that yeast was really understood and controlled. Nowadays yeasts are kept in batches in specific yeast centers.

Hops
In the past before the introduction of hops into the brewing process all kinds of different herbs and spices and fruits were used to flavor and preserve the beer. Some countries (Belgium, Britain) never really stopped using them and still use them today, whilst others passed purity laws (*Reinheitsgebot*) expressly forbidding any other adjuncts except the aromatic hop. Although known since ancient times (related to the nettle and first cousin to cannabis) and used in a variety of purposes, the combination of hops with malts in beer production dates back to the Weihenstephan breweries in Bavaria. It took time for the practice to spread and they were not in regular use in Britain until around the fifteenth century. It is the female hop that is used for brewing. Containing resins, essential oils, tannins, and preservatives, hops have a range of effects when combined with malts in the brewing process. They give aroma, flavor, have preservative properties, and add bitterness.

Fermentation.
The oldest method of brewing beer is top fermentation. In this method the yeasts are allowed to rise to the top of the fermenting beer. Fermentation takes place at a highish temperature (15-20°C or above) and over a short period of time—only three to five days. Alternatively, bottom fermentation has become the most widely used process and is used in the making of lager. The temperature at which

fermentation takes place in this method is consequently lower (6-8°C) and the time taken is considerably longer—seven to ten days.

It is during fermentation that the alcohol content develops. The level of alcohol depends on the initial sugar level in the wort and the extent to which it is fermented, often called attenuation—the function of time against the conversion of sugar into alcohol.

Conditioning.
Following fermentation, the "green" (as young beer is called) is then decanted into kegs, barrels or bottles to be conditioned. At this point more ingredients may be added to "tweak" the brew and continue fermentation—usually more fermentable material (for example, wort for Kräusen), yeast or hops. This process can last anything from between a week to up to two years, depending on which style of beer is being made. This time variation is yet another important stage which affects the flavor and taste of the finished product. Ales and stouts are not normally stored for long, whereas lager (the name originating from the German word for "store") is laid down for a longer period.

Beer Strength
The strength, or alcoholic content, of every beer is given as part of the information on the label. This figure is not quite as straightforward as it appears when it comes to comparing one brand against another. This is because different countries use different ways to present the alcoholic information. For example, in most of Europe the strength of beer is presented in terms of the percentage of alcohol by volume (exactly the same way as wine). However, generally across the United States the same information is presented as alcohol by weight. Most beers come in around 4–5% by volume (AbV); specialized brews have a higher rating, usually between 6 and 8%.

BEER TYPES

ALES
Term used for top-fermenting beers of English styles with sign of fruitiness. Produced in a variety of aromas, strengths, and colors.

Barley Wine
Extra-strong ale (up to the strength of wine). Usually darker, but pale version can be found.

American Barley Wine tends to be hoppier than traditional European examples.

Bitter
British-style hopped ale, such as Morland's Old Speckled Hen (*Right*). Bitters tend to show some hop bitterness with colors ranging from light pale to dark copper. Alcohol content from 3.5 to 4.5 for "Best" and "Special."

Blonde Ale
All-malt beer with pleasant hop bouquet and soft lightly malted palate and some fruitiness. Blonde Ales are often lager-like and appeal to non-ale drinkers in brewpubs and micro-breweries.

Brown Ale
Sweeter, fuller-bodied and lighter in color than standard English milds. Low in bitterness and depending on origin some nutty character.

India Pale Ale
Traditionally a style brewed for consumption in the Indian Empire with high hop rates of Fuggles and Golding hops for preservation and strength to survive the long journey. Today often paler than the classic Pale Ale. IPA should be of medium body and medium maltiness to cover the higher alcohol contents of 5.5–7%. American craftsbrewers tend to brew hoppier version.

Mild Ale
Originating from the mining areas of England with low alcohol and lack of bitterness. In general sweeter and paler than porter, but with sufficient malt body. Around 3% AbV.

Pale Ale
Often used interchangeably with the term "Bitter" and used by some brewers to identify their premium bitters. Pale color ranges from light amber to copper.

Porter
Old London-style ale which has seen some revival in recent years. Full-bodied with coffee-like dryness from use of dark roasted and chocolate malts. In color reddish-brown to black. Some versions are made from bottom-fermenting yeast.

Scottish Ale
Maltier flavor and aroma compared to English ales. Can be found in various versions: Light, Heavy, Export, and Strong or by their old taxation ratings 60/- (shillings), 70/-, 80/-, and 90/-.

STOUTS
Originally the Irish version of London Porter. A dry, extra-dark top-fermented brew with highly roasted barley and malt.

Dry Stout
Irish style as typified by Guinness around the world. Medium to high bitterness brew which has sometimes unmalted barley added to sweeten hop bitterness.

Imperial Stout
Originally brewed as a robust and stronger dry stout for export to Russia. High alcohol content with noticeable esters and fruitiness. Often with an intense "burnt currant" or coffee flavor. Between 7–9+% AbV.

Milk Stout
English version of the stout with an overall sweet character. Flavor derived from use of milk sugar (lactose) and chocolate malt. Beers have no hop aroma and are low alcohol of 3% AbV.

Oatmeal Stout
Variation of English stout with added oatmeal to increase body and flavor. Hint of nuttiness with some caramel flavors.

LAGERS
Generic term for all bottom-fermenting beers. Usually golden in color and darker version prominent in Continental Europe and the USA.

Pils/Pilsner
Often used to describe any golden-colored, dry, bottom-fermented beer sometimes implying premium quality. Originating from Pilsen as the Pilsner Urquell (= original source) the style should be characterized by a good hoppiness with flowery aroma and dry finish. German Pilsner are more bitter,   less malty, and cleaner in taste than the Bohemian originals.

Bock
Very strong lager originating from Einbeck, North Germany. Although strong in alcohol (6–7.5% AbV) it is clean tasting with malty sweet character and low bitterness. Also a term used as indication for strength, e.g. Weizenbock.

Doppelbock
Any stronger version of bock (over 7.5% AbV) has to be called Doppelbock. Very full-bodied, dark gold to very dark brown, with balanced bitterness.

Eisbock
Traditional type of bock (not to be confused with Ice Beer). Produced by freezing Doppelbock and removing the ice leaving behind a higher concentration of alcohol of 10–14% AbV.

Märzen/Oktoberfest Lager
Lager produced in Bavaria as as adaptation of Vienna lager with malt sweetness and malt aroma. Medium body with low to medium hop bitterness. Traditionally produced in March, when legislation and lack of refrigeration prohibited brewing during the summer.

Vienna Lager
Classic amber lager style. Distinctive character due to malting process which produces the toasty flavor and color.

Malt Liquor
Rather ambiguous American term for stronger variation of standard American lager. Some states require all beers over 5% AbV to be labeled Malt Liquor.

American Standard
Brewed with 25–40% rice and corn. Very low in malt aroma and flavors. Lightly hopped and light-bodied.

Wheat Beer
Highly effervescent, top-fermented brew using over 50% wheat with little hop character.

Bavarian Wheat beer
Light to medium body with fruity flavors. Flavors can include bananas, vanilla, cloves, nutmeg, and cinnamon. Some bubble gum may be detected in

fresh beers. Can be called Hefe (Yeast)—Weiss, Weizen or Weisse. Kristall denotes a filtered wheat beer.

Belgian Wheat beer/Wit

Orange and spicy taste characterizes this style. Although orange peel is commonly used it is the type of yeast that is mainly responsible for orange/citrus aromas. The beer is brewed with quantities of unmalted wheat which gives it a fuller body and more graininess than German Wheat beers.

SPECIALITY BEERS

Altbier

From northern Germany, this is a top-fermenting beer. "Alt," meaning old in German, was used to make it clear that this was not a lager, but rather a beer made in the old-fashioned way. Altbier is warm-fermented, followed by a cold maturation period. The clean-tasting, hoppy, somewhat bitter finish has become popular in the United States.

Bière de Garde

From northern France, these beers were originally brewed in late winter to be drunk the following summer. They are medium-strong in alcohol with a spicy fruitiness. Originally top-fermenting, they were developed in farmhouse breweries: now Bière de garde is commercially brewed, though still not widely available outside northern France and southern Belgium.

Kölsch

Beer from Cologne (Köln) which has been given legal protection meaning that only the Cologne Association of Brewers (in Cologne and locality) can make this delicate, pale golden beer. Top-fermented, cold-matured, and filtered to produce a delicate, medium strength, clean tasting, rather hoppy beer.

Steam Beer

Classically, this is an American West Coast—specifically San Francisco—speciality. The brew is fermented in shallow vessels at ale temperatures with a lager yeast to allow it to cool faster in the hot climate. This gives the beer its own distinct character.

Trappist Beers

Only six Trappist monasteries still make beer, these are Orval, Rochefort, Chimay, Westmalle, and Sint Sixtus in Belgium, and Schaapskooi in the Netherlands. As can be expected from such an old tradition, the brews are all strong, usually sweet and always fruity and aromatic. They are top-fermented and bottle-conditioned.

Abbey Beers

These were originally made in Belgium by religious orders other than Trappists. Nowadays they are largely made under license by commercial breweries. Abbey-style beers are now brewed in an increasing number of microbreweries in the United States.

Faro

This is a type of Lambic beer, made from a young brew which has been sweetened with molasses, sugar or caramel and sometimes also spiced. The resulting brew is pasteurized to prevent the sugar from fermenting. It is a light, sweet, drink traditionally watered down for easy drinking.

Gueuze

Blend of young and old lambic to create bottle-conditioned beer of light gold to amber color. No sugar or yeast is added. Matures in bottles up to several years. Unfortunately, some commercial examples available today are very much considered "untrue to the style."

Lambic

Sour wheat beer made by fermentation with wild yeast in a small region around Brussels. After primary fermentation it is stored for up to three years in wooden barrels undergoing secondary fermentation.

Rauchbier

A dark, bottom-fermented beer made from grain malted by being spread out over a fine mesh to dry in a kiln heated by a wood fire. In the process the grains develop a dry and smoky taste. This traditional method of drying grain has largely died out everywhere except Poland and Germany. (Scotch whisky also uses this method.)

Winter/Seasonal

As the name implies, these are produced to coincide with a particular season—usually in the cold winter months. Consequently they tend to be full-bodied, strong, and on the sweet side.

Anchor Steam Beer

Brewery: Anchor Brewing Company

Address: 1705 Mariposa Street
San Francisco
California 94107
USA

Telephone: 415 863 8350

Originally founded in 1890, bought out when bankrupt by Fritz Maytag in 1965 and now one of the most successful and admired breweries in the United States, the Anchor Brewing Co's prime product is Anchor Steam Beer, made by a process unique to the USA. Before refrigeration was available in the West, brewers used lager yeasts at normal temperatures in very shallow fermenting vessels. The resulting beer possesses the full roundness of a lager with the fruity tang of an ale, and high carbonation. An all-malt beer, with a hoppy dryness, its AbV is 5.0%.

Anchor also makes Porter, a rich creamy bottom-fermented stout, Liberty Ale (6.0% AbV), which is top-fermented, and aromatic with a dry and hoppy finish, a barley wine (Old Foghorn), fruity wheat beers, and Our Special Ale, a winter warmer produced between Thanksgiving and New Year, each year's brew having a different tree on the label.

Asahi

Brewery: Asahi Breweries

Address: 23-1 Azmabashi 1-Chome
Sumida-ku
Tokyo
130 Japan

Telephone: 03 5608 5112

Since Western style beers were introduced into Japan in the nineteenth century they have continued to increase in popularity and demand. The Japanese brewing industry is one of the most technologically advanced in the world and now it too is expanding rapidly with the growth of micro-breweries and brewpubs. Asahi is one of the big four national brewers—the other three are the giant Kirin (one of the top five world beer producers), Sapporo, and Suntory—who make an ever-increasing range of beers.

Asahi is known for its Draft Super Dry Pilsner, a pale dry draft cold-filtered beer for all seasons of 5.0% AbV. This beer caused a huge sensation when it came out, so big that it was named the 'Dry Boom' in Japan. Dry beer is made by using corn and rice with enzymes and super-attenuating yeast; as a result, the beer ferments more completely and has less residual sweetness. The result is a sharp dry taste—one of the most loved beers in Japan although beer experts of other countries give it mixed reviews.

Asahi also makes Draft Pilsner—with a slightly nutty flavor—the remarkable Asahi Stout (8% AbV), a true top-fermented beer. Brewed only occasionally, it has a large full flavor with hints of fruit and hops.

Asahi—as with all the major Japanese brewers—also makes a German-style Black Beer; at 5% AbV it has a sweet aroma and flavor of malt and caramel.

Aecht Schlenkerla Rauchbier

Brewer: Brauerei Heller-Trum

Address: Schlenkerla
6 Dominikaner Strasse
D-96049 Bamberg
Germany

Telephone: 0951 56060

The smoky beers of the Bamberg region hark back to the past, taking their character from the method they use to kiln malt—over beechwood fires. The town is famous for its malts and breweries, following a tradition lost to many others and they still smoke their barley malt over beechwood fires.

Heller-Trum is a classic brewer of this style, with a long history dating back to its beginnings brewing in the Schlenkerla tavern in 1678. The beer was lagered (stored) in caves in the surrounding hills until demand forced them to move to bigger premises.

The main beer produced is a Rauchbier called Aecht Schlenkerla (4.8 AbV), where "Aecht" is translated as "Real" and "Schlenkerla" is after the famous tavern, itself supposedly named an old and ape-like former brewer. To produce Aecht Schlenkerla open-topped copper vessels are used for primary fermentation and the result is then lagered for two months. Aecht Schlenkerla is dark brown-colored, with a smoky malt aroma that gives a dry taste with a smoked and slightly fruity finish. It is classified as a Märzen, as it was originally brewed for the Oktoberfest

The brewery also makes a smoky Bock and a Helles.

Bass Ale

Brewery: Bass Brewers

Address: 137 High Street
Burton-on-Trent
Staffordshire
DE14 1JZ
England

Telephone: 01283 511000

Bass is one of the UK's big three brewers, producing a wide selection of beers ranging from Tennent's lagers to Draught Bass. Over the years Bass has merged with many brewers to form the huge combine it is today, from the big names—such as the other famous Burton brewery, Worthington, in the 1920s or the the merger with Charrington United Breweries—to the small, such as the Younger Brewery of Alloa, Scotland.

Emblazoned on the bottle of Bass's wonderful bitter is a red triangle, which announces another claim to fame: it was Britain's first registered trademark on its pale ale; the second was the red diamond on the front of Bass' No. 1, a barley wine.

Bass pale ales are directly descended from the original pales made for the colonial market. The draught Bass is made at Burton from a single barley malt, using Challenger and Northdown hops and two strains of yeast to give a complex taste and aroma. At 4.4% AbV, it may not be the strongest beer on the market, but there is no doubting its quality and taste, particularly if drunk in the British way (not too cold!).

In Birmingham, Cape Hill produce the best-known bottled Pale Ale: Worthington White Shield, 5.6% AbV—dry, hoppy and fruity with a slight smokiness, it is one of the few bottle-conditioned ales in Britain.

Boddingtons Draught

Brewery: Whitbread Beer Company

Address: Porter Tun House
Capability Green
Luton
Bedfordshire
LU1 3LS
England

Telephone: 0582 391166

Whitbread is one of Britain's largest brewery groups, with a number of famous brands under its wing. Its origins are respectably ancient: Samuel Whitbread, a small London brewer, made his name and fortune by switching production to porter. By 1760 he had built the famous Porter Tun Room in his Chiswell Street premises and vast vats to contain the maturing beer.

Now without a London plant (in 1992 when it wanted to celebrate its 250th anniversary the commemorative porter was brewed in Castle Eden, Co. Durham), Whitbread produces Mackeson, Gold Label, and the beer highlighted here—the, as the advertising slogan would have it, "cream of Manchester."

Boddingtons certainly is Mancunian—it's Manchester's oldest brewery, dating back to 1778. It is very close to the city center and was extensively damaged during World War 2, undergoing a huge reconstruction and modernization program afterwards. The word "creamy" also reflects its draft well—particularly in cans where the revolutionary "widget" gives a very creamy drink. Boddingtons also makes produces a Mild—dark and medium sweet—and a Best Mild which is stronger. Its bottled beers include Boddington Light—a light dinner ale almost like a lager in character, a Strong Ale and, Boddington Nut Brown—a sweet brown ale —and Boddington Extra Stout.

DRAUGHT

DRAUGHTFLOW
SYSTEM

CONTAINS BOTTLE WIDGET

JUL98
211K

ESTABLISHED **BODDINGTONS** SINCE 1778

BREWED TO A UNIQUE NORTHERN RECIPE USING ONLY THE FINEST INGREDIENTS

TRADE   MARK

ALCOHOL 3.8%
BY VOLUME

BREWED IN MANCHESTER

DRAUGHT

Brewed at Boddingtons Brewery, Strangeways, Manchester.
Distributed by The Whitbread Beer Company, Whitbread plc, London EC1Y 4SD.

Brooklyn Lager

Brewery: The Brooklyn Brewery

Address: 79 North 11th Street
Brooklyn
New York 11211
USA

Telephone: 718 486 7422

Once Brooklyn had over 40 breweries, but Prohibition and depression saw them all closed down. The Brooklyn Brewery typifies the resurgence of brewing in the USA. It revived the old New York brewing tradition in the 1980s, although its beers were brewed under contract until its own plant opened in 1996.

The brewery was started by Steve Hindy and Tom Potter—journalist and banker respectively—who called in the assistance of Bill Moeller, a retired, practiced brewer, who helped make a lager (5.1% AbV), which is dry-hopped and brewed from crystal and pale malts. It is a dry, firm lager, possessing a full malty flavor with hints of fruit and flowers, and was specifically brewed—as the beer's slogan "The Pre-Prohibition Beer" suggests—to reproduce the lager-brewing tradition of the days before prohibition.

The company also produces Brooklyn Brown Ale (6% AbV), a top-fermented ale made from crystal, pale, chocolate and black malts that is dry-hopped. It has a chocolatey and coffee-like aroma with a dry nutty finish. Brooklyn also makes a Black Chocolate Stout (8.3% AbV), that has become justly famous. It is brewed from pale and dark malts with a roasted malty chocolate aroma and a dryish hop and chocolate finish.

Brewed
pale an
barley,
Cascade
Please
brewery
Store at
Street, B
USA or fr
www.broo

THE BROOKLYN BREWERY
BROOKLYN NEW YORK

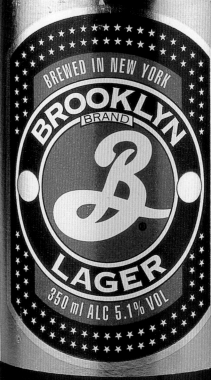

BREWED IN NEW YORK

BROOKLYN
BRAND

B

LAGER

350 ml ALC 5.1% VOL

Budweiser Budvar

Brewery: Budejovice Budvar

Address: Karoliny Svetle 4
370 21 Ceske Budejovice
Czech Republic

Telephone: 0387 705111

In the country of Bohemia, now a region of the Czech Republic, the town of Ceske Budejovice has an ancient brewing tradition; in the fifteenth century the Bohemian Royal Court brewers were one of the 40-odd breweries plying their trade in the town which is better known by its German name—Budweis. Its beers were commonly known as Budweisers, and gained a reputation every bit as substantial as that of Pilsen.

Only two of the many breweries are still in existence today, the Samson Brewery (the Budweiser Bürgerbräu) which dates back to 1795 and that of Budweiser Budvar, which dates from 1895. Both these breweries brew excellent lagers, the latter's 5% AbV, an all-malt beer using Zatec hops, with a rich malty aroma and a hint of vanilla, a hoppy taste and a dry fruity finish. In its preparation a double decoction mash is used, with initial fermentation in open vessels. It is then lagered for three months—a particularly long period, but one that produces a respected beer.

Unfortunately, Budvar cannot be sold in the USA because of legal wrangling with the giant Anheuser-Busch brewery, founded some 25 years earlier than its Bohemian rival. This fact was crucial in determining a legal case which saw the St. Louis Budweiser become the only beer to be legally sold in the USA with that name. However, since the fall of Communism, Anheuser-Busch has made great efforts to buy a stake in the Czech concern, so it is possible that future may see a change in Budvar's availability.

Caledonian 80/- Export Ale

Brewery: Caledonian Brewing Company

Address: 42 Slateford Road
Edinburgh
EH11 1PH
Scotland

Telephone: 0131 337 1286

Originally created in 1869 as Lorimer & Clark to supply the northeast of England, the Caledonian was taken over by Vaux in 1919 and faced closure in 1987, until it was saved by a management buy-out. Thus some of the finest and fullest malt ales brewed in Scotland were safeguarded. We all can enjoy the 80/- (4.1% AbV), rich and malty in flavor, Flying Scotsman (5.1% AbV), a full-flavored ruby ale combining the best of Scottish barley and English hops, and Golden Promise, Britain's first organic ale. Other bottled ales include: Merman XXX (4.8% AbV), an impressively complex beer, with robust interwoven malt with flavors that persist well past the last swallow; and Scotch Ale (7.2% AbV), which has a deep amber-brown color, without the cloying sweetness of other beers of this strength.

Chimay Première

Brewery: Abbaye de Notre-Dame de Scourmont

Address: Rue de la Trappe 294
6438 Forges-les-Chimay
Belgium

Telephone: 060 21 03 11

Chimay Trappist Monastery is the biggest and most famous of the monastery breweries and the first to begin commercial brewing. The monks make their fine ales in traditional top-fermented fashion, using water from their own wells, French and Belgian winter barleys for a pale malt, flavored with Yakima Valley and Hallertauer hops and a yeast strain from a now closed local brewery. In addition some candy sugar is added just prior to bottling for extra fermentation.

Chimay produces three regular ales, each known by the color of its cap and label—Red (7% AbV), the original product, is also called Première and comes in 75cl. bottles.. It is copper-colored with a soft taste and a mild fruity palate. White (8% AbV) is full and firm with a light peachy color, a dry hoppy palate and a spicy, fruity finish. Blue (9% AbV) is vintage-dated, and is the most suited to laying down, or storing, maturing considerably with age. It is the strongest of the three, spicy and peppery, with a fruity aroma and a dry smooth finish. Different vintages are sold in restaurants close to the abbey for the pleasure of beer connoisseurs.

Cooper's Sparkling Ale

Brewery: Cooper's Brewery

Address: 9 Statenborough Street
Leabrook
Adelaide
South Australia 5068
Australia

Telephone: 08 8300 4222

The only large brewery to continue producing traditional ales in the face of the lager revolution that swept Australia, Cooper's products are now recognized and enjoyed worldwide. Founded by Methodist Thomas Cooper, who emigrated with his family from Yorkshire in 1852, the firm was founded in 1862 and is still family-run.

Its ales include the best-known Sparkling Ale (5.8% AbV), an old-fashioned top-fermented ale with a distinct copper color, and a hoppy aroma, brewed from pale and crystal malts with cane sugar added, and Pride of Ringwood hops. Initial fermentation was originally in open wooden vessels, but the company now uses conical ones. The beer is then centrifuged, with more wort and sugar being added to promote a secondary fermentation in the bottle. The result is intense, flavorsome and—despite the name—cloudy with yeast from secondary fermentation.

Other Cooper's brews are the classic Stout (6.8% AbV), which consists of a roasted malt added to paler and crystal ones, with an aroma reminiscent of coffee; Cooper's Dark (4.5% AbV) is made from a combination of pale, crystal and roasted malts, and possesses a fruity character.

Diebels Alt

Brewer: Privatbrauerei Diebels GMBH

Address: Brauerei-Diebels Strasse 1
47661 Issum
Düsseldorf
Germany

Telephone: 02835 300

The Diebels Altbier—announced as German Premium Beer on export bottles—is manufactured in northwestern Germany by a company which runs one of the oldest family breweries in Germany from a small hamlet called Issum: it is also one of the larger beer producers in the country. Diebels Alt (or Old) beer is named after the old method of top fermentation, which so many brewers stopped using with the introduction of lager brewing in the nineteenth century. In the area around Düsseldorf the tradition of Altbier brewing has continued unbroken, with many rich dark malty ales brewed and served locally, often getting their color from Vienna or black malts. Originally destined to quench the thirst of the miners and steelworkers of the area, the best way of getting the taste for these brews is to wander the cobbled streets of Düsseldorf Alt Stadt and visit the excellent brewpubs, such as Zum Uerige or Im Füchschen!

Diebels also produces Altbier in bottles, using a Pilsner malt with 2% roasted barley, Perle and Northern Brewer hops and a 50-year old top-fermenting yeast strain. The result is a good copper-colored beer of 4.8% AbV with a malty aroma, a slightly bitter taste and a nutty, dry finish with a hint of fruit.

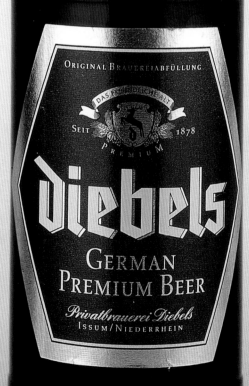

Dos Equis

Brewery: Cervecaria Moctezuma

Address: 156 Lago Alberto
Mexico City 11320
Mexico

Telephone: 525 670 4243

The original name of this beer was "Siglo XX," a name which referred to the century of manufacture. Today this has been shortened to "Dos Equis," which—as the logo on the bottle indicates—means two crosses and alludes to the crosses marked on casks when beer was blessed. The name is given to a dark amber lager (4.8% AbV) in the Viennese style, with a rich fruity aroma and taste, and a light dry chocolate and hop finish which has substantially more character and flavor than many of the insipid Latin American lagers.

Dos Equis has been brewed since 1900, first by Cervecaria Moctezuma in the city of Orizaba, Veracruz, in southern Mexico. It is now brewed by the huge Moctezuma-Cuauhtemoc group, the biggest brewer in Mexico, which is also responsible for Sol (see page 80) and other brews such as another lager more in the Pilsner tradition called Bohemia. A lager-type beer, characterized by its amber hue and its excellent quality, which guarantees an outstanding soft aroma and a balanced taste of malt and hops, Dos Equis has a strong taste, full body and intense color, making it a fine accompaniment to any meal. It is available for the export market, being sold in more than 30 different countries.

DOS EQUIS

XX

BEER·BIER·BIRRA·BIERE
CERVEZA

33 cl

4.8% alc./vol.

BREWED AND BOTTLED BY CERVECERIA MOCTEZUMA, S.A. DE C.V.
ORIZABA, VER. MEXICO, PRODUCT OF MEXICO, MARC. REG. Reg. S.S.A. 4859°8°

Duvel

Brewery: Moortgat Brewery

Address: 58 Breendonk Dorp
2659 Puurs
Belgium

Telephone: 03 886 7121

The Moortgat brewery was founded 1871, and produced good, workmanlike brews—including Scotch ales and Pilseners as fashion dictated but its famous Duvel brand was not brewed until one hundred years after the brewery opened, in 1971. The name means "Devil" and is Flemish and so pronounced "Doovel." There is an interesting story behind its name—according to legend, a brewery worker exclaimed after first tasting it, "This is a devil of a beer," and the name stuck. Cleverly used in advertising, there have been imitators since, but none has reached the quality level of Duvel.

Moortgat is a family-run brewery which uses its own malts combined with Styrian and Saaz hops and two different strains of yeast. Duvel has a complicated brewing process, undergoing both cold and warm maturation and it is then bottled and stored for a month, where it undergoes a third fermentation. A sparkling pale golden beer with a full head and the deceptive color of lager, it is all-malt and top-fermented, and has a soft beguiling delicate taste—clean, smooth and slightly fruity, that belies its strong effect (8.5% AbV).

Serving Duvel puts one between the devil and the deep blue sea: should it be served ice cold, with the glass chilled or at a natural cellar temperature? Both ways are entirely possible and do not hide its clear "Poire Willem" (pear brandy) bouquet.

Einbecker Mai-Ur-Bock

Brewer: Einbecker Brauhaus

Address: 4-7 Papen Strasse
37574 Einbeck
Lower Saxony
Germany

Telephone: 05561 7970

In the 14th century, Einbeck, with its 700 brewing locations, was the center of the brewing world. There were, however, only 10 officially recognized brewmasters in the town who wandered, together with their serf-like helpers and brewing pots, from household to household. In 1612, the best Einbeck brewmaster was hired away by the newly built Munich Hofbräuhaus. This master brewer brought his recipe for

"Einbecksche" with him. From this name, soon changed to "Oan Pockisch" in Bavarian German, then to "Oan Pock", came finally today's "Bock," which can be dark or pale and in various forms—Doppelbock, Maibock, and Eisbock. Bocks are bottom-fermented and quite strong.

This brewery produces three styles of Bock, all with full malty aromas and hoppy dry finishes. Hell is the lighter version, Dunkel is more rounded, and the seasonal Maibock, available from March to May, is a refreshing clean tasting brew, with a slight malty dryness in its finish.

Freedom Premium Pilsener

Brewery: The Freedom Brewing Co Ltd

Address: The Coachworks
80 Parson's Green Lane
Fulham
London SW6 4HU
England

Telephone: 0171 731 7372

The Freedom Brewing Company, the UK's first and only lager microbrewery, may only have been founded in 1995 but the hand-crafted beer it produces, Freedom Premium Pilsener (5% AbV), is consistently rated the best bottled lager brewed in the UK.

Freedom is a magical combination of Bavarian yeast, Czech and American hops, and English malt. The centuries-old strain of yeast, brought by hand from the Spaten Brauerei, is bottom-fermenting. The hops used are a blend of Liberty hops from North West America—an aromatic variety which shares the prized characteristics of the renowned Hallertauer Hersbrücker and yet also enjoys a distinctively individual fragrance—and the world famous Saaz hops from the Czech Republic. The malted barley, Maris Otter from East Anglia, is floor-malted in the traditional manner and is justifiably acknowledged throughout the brewing world as one of the finest quality malts available today.

Using these outstanding ingredients, Freedom is brewed with ten days' chilled fermentation followed by four to six weeks' lagering at -2°C (which is unique in the UK), in accordance with the strict demands of the *Reinheitsgebot* (the German Purity Beer Law of 1516). To retain its distinctive contemporary taste Freedom is not pasteurized and the brewery prides itself on delivering to its clients immediately after filtration and bottling.

Golden Gate Original Ale

Brewery: Golden Pacific Brewing Company

Address: 1404 Fourth Street
Berkeley
California 94710
USA

Telephone: 510 558 1919

The great revival in American beer which saw hundreds of microbreweries and brew-pubs start up might—as is only natural—be retrenching somewhat, but it has rekindled an interest in taste which will not go away, no matter how hard the big concerns may peddle their blander mass-market goods.

The majority of new beers produced in the United States are ales, getting back to the original beers which reached the New World through European immigrants before the lager revolution. While fewer American companies have taken up brown ale, a number have, some going to the extreme of taking the description "nut brown" literally and adding nuts!

Golden Gate Original Brown Ale (5.7% AbV) is a splendid, full-bodied, fruity example of the type and comes from one of the many thriving breweries located in the San Francisco area—the Golden Pacific Brewing Company, which is a microbrewery producing about 7,200 barrels annually. It moved from Emeryville to Berkeley in early 1997 and seems set fair to continue production of a range of beers which include: Golden Bear lager, Golden Gate Original, Pale Ale, Copper Ale; and the seasonal Hybernator, which 6.5% AbV.

in small batches,
by people who
love brewing and
sharing great beer.

GOLDEN GATE

A classic American style ale: big and
full-bodied yet delightfully refreshing. Rich
malt undertones and bright Yakima Valley
hops create an always intriguing character.

ORIGINAL ALE

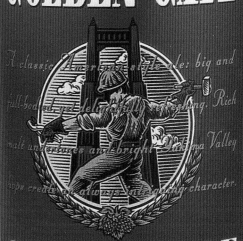

Grolsch Premium Lager

Brewery: Grolsche Bierbrouwerij

Address: Eibergsweg 10
7141 CE Groenlo
Holland

Telephone: 053 483 3333

As with so many of today's successful breweries, the taste and flavor of the beer is not always the main reason for its success—it has to be cleverly advertised and packaged. Grolsch is both of those: who can forget the old-fashioned earthenware stopper? Until recently a small brewer in a small Dutch town of Grolle, Grolsche is now Holland's major independent and world famous for its fresh, crisp, premium lager and, increasingly, for its other more recent variations.

Grolsch—a Pilsener-type lager—is made from a selection of malts from five different countries—Holland, England, Belgium, France and Germany, and is flavored with Saaz and Hallertauer hops. A small amount of maize is added in the malt grist, to produce a distinctive and well-balanced flavor—although these changes vary around the world depending on the brewer, because it is is brewed outside Holland under licence, in England by Bass.

Grolsche now has a second brewery—in Entschede—and as well as Grolsch Pilsener (which is what Premium is called in Holland) also produces a sharp and creamy Dark (Bok) Lager, with a roasted malty flavor; a crisp, fresh Dry Draft (Mei Bok) Pilsner; and Grolsch Amber—a very different product altogether! In style like an Altbier, Amber is a very pleasant brew, all-malt with some wheat malt added to keep the head. It is recommended.

Guinness Original

Brewery: Guinness Ireland Group Ltd

Address: St James's Gate Brewery
Dublin 8
Ireland

Telephone: 01 453 6700

Ireland's most famous export was founded in 1759 by Arthur Guinness, who bought a disused abbey brewery in Dublin. Despite the problems of famine and depopulation over the next century, Guinness continued to brew ales and then porters which were transported countrywide using the canal and railway networks. Ultimately the porter name was dropped and Guinness beers were known simply as stout.

Following adventurous sales campaigns and Irish immigration, Guinness made an impact worldwide, and by the turn of the century it was the largest brewing concern in the world. The success—and the advertising!— continued and the Guinness expanded, building breweries in England (Park Royal, London) and later unsuccessfully in the US

Guinness has lost a great deal of its fruitiness over time, yet remains one of the driest of stouts. There are at present nineteen different versions brewed, ranging from draft to bottled, using a barley malt and a blend of English and American hops. The same strain of yeast as Arthur Guinness' original is still used. It works at a temperature of 25°C, fermenting rapidly in just two to four days.

The bottled Guinness Original is allowed to ferment a second time by adding wort to the already fermented beer in the bottle. Irish Draught Guinness has the same strength as Original (4.1% AbV). Export Draught is stronger (5.0%AbV), the bottled Guinness brewed in Dublin for the Belgian market is stronger still (8.0AbV)! Perhaps the most interesting version is Foreign Extra Stout (7.5%AbV), which is stored in a pair of 18th century oak vats saved from the first Guinness brewery.

Heineken Export

Brewery: Heineken NV

Address: Tweede Weteringplantsoen 21
1017ZD Amsterdam
Netherlands

Telephone: 020 523 9239

Headquartered in Amsterdam, Heineken is one of the biggest brewing concerns in the world—second in annual production to Anheuser-Busch—and the largest importer into the United States, with technical involvement in 100 overseas breweries. Its origins date back to 1863, when Gerard Heineken bought the largest brewery in Amsterdam—De Hooiberg, which dated back at least to the sixteenth century. Since then Heineken has gone from strength to strength, merging with or taking over a number of its competitors over the years—such as Amstel or Brand, the oldest Dutch brewery dating back to the fourteenth century.

Heineken produces a variety of famous beers, in recent years concentrating on high-volume production of bottled lagers: the most widely known being a clean, crisp Pilsener (5.0% AbV), which is sometimes criticized for blandness, but is still one of the world's favorite lagers.

Other Heineken beers include Tarwebok (5.0% AbV), a seasonal speciality beer which contains 17% percent of wheat and possesses a complex fruity character with a hint of chocolate. Amstel beers tend to be fuller than Heineken, with a lighter aroma and a hoppy flavor: there's the straightforward Amstel Bier (5.0% AbV), Amstel Gold, strong and hoppy (7.0% AbV) and Amstel Bock, another seasonal speciality with a full malty flavor (7.0% AbV). Heineken also owns Murphy's in Ireland, brewer of the famous Irish Stout (4.3%AbV).

Hoegaarden Bière Blanche/Wit

Brewery: Brouwerij De Kluis

Address: Stoopkensstraat 46
3320 Hoegaarden
Brabant
Belgium

Telephone: 016 76 7676

The region of Brabant in Belgium once had over 30 breweries making wheat beers, famous for their distinctive additions of herbs, spices and fruit. These had slowly declined with the last closing only after World War 2. Then in the 1960s an independent brewer called Pierre Celis revived the style, calling his brewery De Kluis (The Cloister) in memory of the monks who had pioneered the process. His Hoegaarden became one of the main leaders of the resurgence of white beers.

Hoegaarden is, at 5.0% AbV, made from an equal mixture of unmalted barley and raw wheat, spiced with coriander and curacao. A top-fermenting strain of yeast is used, with further priming of yeast and a little sugar added just before bottling for a secondary fermentation in the bottle. The resulting beer is cloudy white with a spicy aroma and a clean fruity finish.

Hoegaarden also makes Grand Cru, (8.7 AbV), a spiced beer using only malted barley. It has a warm full-bodied texture and a well balanced taste. Also produced is Verboden Vrucht (Forbidden Fruit), a fine all-malt ruby colored beer of 9.0% AbV made with Styrian and Challenger hops and added coriander to give a spicy, fruity strong ale. Hoegaarden was taken over by the brewing giant Interbrew and founding father Pierre Celis set up in the US in 1992; his Austin-based brewery was subsequently bought out by Miller and the brilliant Celis returned to Europe.

Kingfisher

Brewery: United Breweries Group Ltd

Address: Bangalore
India

Telephone: 812 21 4548

There are over seventy different varieties of the striking riverside-living Kingfisher in the Indian subcontinent, but there's only one Kingfisher lager, India's top selling brand with nearly 25% of a market which, at a potential 900 million, is a substantial one!

Kingfisher is a sweet malty lager (4.8% AbV) with a barley presence and only slight hop nuances; it is lagered for a minimum of eight weeks. Cool and refreshing ("most thrilling chilled"), it complements Indian food magnificently, especially hot curries, and is sold in more than 6,500 of the 7,000 UK Indian restaurants.

Kingfisher is the flagship brand of United Breweries (U. B.), headquartered today at Bangalore. U. B. was started in 1857 with Castle Breweries. In 1915 Scotsman Thomas Leishman combined Castle and four other South India breweries to form U.B. and today it is a substantial international conglomerate with 13 breweries in India and operations in 20 countries, including all the major beer markets worldwide—a far cry from its modest beginnings. Indeed, Kingfisher today is available in 31 countries and is brewed in Britain under licence by Shepherd Neame, from where North American exports originate. Shepherd Neame-brewed Kingfisher won the Gold Medal in the Pale Lager Class at the 1997 Chicago World Beer Championships, to add to two consecutive best lager awards in Sweden in 1994 and 1995. U. B. also produce U. B. Export and Kalyani.

Labatt Ice

Brewery: Labatt Breweries of Canada

Address: 150 Simcoe Street
London
Ontario N6A 4M3
Canada

Telephone: 519 663 5050

Labatt is the biggest of the three largest brewers in Canada (the others being Carling and Molson), although actually owned by Belgian giant Interbrew since 1995. Labatt owns Rolling Rock—a producer of an eponymous lager in Pittsburg, USA—and Birra Moretti, Peroni's main competitor in Italy.

Labatt's beer is fresh and sweet, and comes in a variety of forms—Blue lager, Classic lager, IPA, Duffy's red ale, Porter, Schooner, Kokanee and, of course, Ice, which was created in 1993 and is one of the company's premier brands. It has been carefully developed, packaged, and promoted to cater for modern drinking tastes: it was the first of this style of drink and set the benchmark for its many imitators.

Ice is rapidly brewed and during the process its temperature is allowed to drop so low that ice particles form; these and other unwanted proteins are removed through a vigorous filtering process. The resulting brew is crystal clear and sharp, almost thin-tasting, although high in alcohol at 5.0% AbV. Interestingly, owing to a national law preventing the export of beer over provincial boundaries (intended to protect small breweries), Labatt's in common with the other large brewers, brews across Canada. Labatt's Ice is therefore brewed in Edmonton, Alberta; St John's, Newfoundland; Halifax, Nova Scotia; and New Westminster, British Columbia, as well as at London, Ontario.

Liefman's Kriek

Brewery: Brouwerij Liefman's NV

Address: Aalst Straat 200
9700 Oudenaarde
Belgium

Telephone: 055 31 13 91

While not unusual in wine-making, it seems very strange to add fruit to beer: but that's just what happens when, once a year, Liefman's adds cherries and raspberries to brown ale rather than the more usual lambic.

Founded in 1679 at Oudenaarde, East Flanders, since the 1990s Liefman's has been part of the Riva group (based in Dentergem, West Flanders). The brewery produces original brown beers, similar to English ones—top-fermenting yeasts are used, with the wort being simmered overnight—and it is also the leading producer of speciality fruit beers. Mashing and brewing take place in West Flanders before the top-fermenting yeast is added at the old brewery at Oudenaarde.

Liefman's produces Oud Bruin (5% AbV), a basic brown beer, brewed from a blend of Munich, Pilsner, and Vienna malts and a variety of English, Czech and German hops; Goudenband (8% AbV), a stronger, more sophisticated version, which has extra yeast and undergoes additional maturation of six to eight months, to produce a rich, complex beer with hints of fruit and spice and a dry hoppy finish. Once a year, at harvest time, cherries and raspberries are added to Goudenband along with extra yeast. This unique use of fresh fruits where others use syrups for flavoring produces two specialty fruit beers—Kriek 6.5% AbV) and Frambozen (4.5% AbV). Individually hand-wrapped, the beer used to be bottled in used half champagne bottles bought from Parisian restaurants.

Marston's Pedigree

Brewery: Marston, Thompson, and Evershead

Address: Shobnall Road
Burton-upon-Trent
Staffordshire
England

Telephone: 01283 531131

John Marston built his brewery in Burton on Trent in 1834. It was the height of the pale ale revolution that saw lighter, hoppy beers replace dark porters and stouts in popularity, and the center of British brewing switch from London to Burton.

The small East Midlands town, famous for its beers since the early middle ages, has remarkable water in the wells and springs that dot the Trent Valley—rich in gypsum and magnesium salts that give a crisp sparkle to pale ales, intensify hop bitterness, and encourage a powerful fermentation.

Marston's today remains a potent link with the hey-day of British brewing. It is still the only brewery in Burton—indeed, the only brewery in the world—using the "union room" method of fermentation in a linked series of oak casks. It is this that gives Marston's Pedigree, the flagship brew, its complex and subtle characteristics.

Pedigree, a 4.5% AbV bitter, is the traditional quaffing ale, a golden pale ale, with a delicate balance of malt and a full but not astringent flavor, Pedigree has a dry hop aroma, but with a full range of all the complex flavors associated with Burton—dryness, drinkability, and just a hint of sulphur character. It is one of Marston's three main brands—the others are Marston's Bitter and Owd Rodger.

Molson

Brewery: Molson Breweries

Address: 175 Bloor Street East,
North Tower,
Toronto
Ontario M4W 3SS4
Canada

Telephone: 416 226 1786

One of the big Canadian brewing giants, Molson merged with Carling in 1989 and also has shares in other big internationals. It can boast of being North America's longest established brewery as it was founded in 1782 by an Englishman. Indeed, it still more closely produces British style beers than other similar big brewers. This is despite the long closure of Canadian breweries—between 1914 and 1932—when the Canadian government enforced a prohibition that less well-publicized, but equally restrictive as that in the United States.

In 1993 Molson introduced the Molson Signature series of all-malt speciality brews. These include Amber Lager (solid and malty), Cream Ale (light-colored, smooth and fruity, with a dry finish), Golden (light and fruity), Export (light, with a touch of fruit and spice), Stock Ale (with a hoppy finish), Rickard"s Nutbrown (thin body with a slight caramel/coffee flavor),Brador (a malt liquor).

Lagers include Molson Canadian (well balanced with a clean dry finish), Carling Black Label (slightly sharp), Old Vienna (slightly sweet), and Molson Ice (crisp and fruity, with a scented aroma).

ESTD 🌿 1786

MOLSON
Smooth
Premium Beer

*For over 200 years Molson has been advancing the
art of brewing. Molson Dry is brewed longer to deliver
a distinctive smooth flavour with a clean crisp finish.*

alc. 5% vol. DRY BREWED FOR SMOOTHNESS 330ml

Newcastle Brown Ale

Brewery: Scottish and Newcastle Breweries

Address: Tyne Brewery
Gallowgate
Newcastle upon Tyne NE99 1RA
England

Telephone: 0191 232 5091

Newcastle Brown is the biggest-selling bottled ale within Britain, and is exported in bottles worldwide. It is a brown ale, a type originally produced as a rival for the paler ales which originated in and around the East Midlands of central England. It is brewed by one of the great breweries of northeastern England—Scottish and Newcastle Beweries, formed in 1960 when Newcastle Breweries merged with the McEwan's and Younger's from across the border in Scotland. The resulting brewing giant is one of the largest and most influential drinks groups in Britain.

First brewed by Colonel Porter in the 1920s, Newcastle Brown was launched in 1927. It is a blend of two beers specifically made for it—one dark brown, the other a pale amber—and a complex combination of four different kinds of hops. To this are added crystal malts and caramel. The end result is a very distinctive, dark browny-red, smooth, sweet, fairly strong (4.7% AbV) malty brew that gained instant popularity. Today, Newcastle Brown is a fundamental part of Tyneside's characteristic ambience—particularly since its logo has been emblazoned in sponsorship on the shirts of Premiership football team Newcastle United.

Peroni Nastro Azzurro

Brewery: Birra Peroni Industriale

Address: Via Mantova 24
1 - 00198 Roma
Italy

Telephone: 0685 4571

Peroni brews Nastro Azzurro and Raffo, both fresh, light, well-balanced Pilseners. Nastro Azzurro—which means Blue Riband—is a premium pale export lager which came into being in 1964 at the Naples brewery, and in 1965 won, as a lager, the World Choice of Beers that took place in Perugia. And still today, more than thirty years from its birth, its dry taste, with the delicate scent of hops, is highly prized by consumers. The straw-yellow Nastro Azzurro has an alcohol content of 5.2% by weight.

Peroni has its roots in Vigevano where it was founded in 1846. Today many of Peroni's beers are brewed in the five breweries of the Peroni Group.—in Padua, Rome, Naples, Battipaglia, and Bari—in addition to these concerns Peroni has a vast warehouse in San Cipriano Po, in the province of Pavia. The production data of the Peroni Group is impressive: from the mash rooms up to 280,000 litres of wort per day can go out; the bottling capacity of the group is 400,000 bottles per hour, 110,000 cans per hour, and 1,800 draft kegs per hour; the stocking capacity in the warehouses is 60,000,000 litres of beer. All this makes for a substantial position in both the Italian and world beer markets.

Pilsner Urquell

Brewery: Urquell Brewery

Address: Plzensky Prazdroj
30497 Plzen
Czech Republic

Telephone: 019 706 1111

Pilsner Urquell was the world's first and greatest golden lager, full of complex malt and hop flavors, though its character has been reduced somewhat since the brewery's wooden fermenters and lagering vessels have been replaced by modern stainless steel ones. This has changed the brewing process and the result, making its complex aroma and taste simpler and perhaps more similar to the German Pilsners—drier and more bitter. However, the delicious, soft, local spring water actually sourced on site at the brewery, is still a constant, as are the flowering heads of three different varieties of Saaz hops, which are used to add their distinct flavor. Pilsner Urquell is still an outstanding lager with crisp fresh creaminess, and is sold around the world

Its name identifies the drink as the original Pilsner, as opposed to the myriad imitations: "Pilsner"—meaning "from Pilsen" in what used to be Bohemia—and "urquell" meaning "original source." The drink's heritage predates the brewing rights granted to Pilsen in 1295 by King Wenceslas .

Sadly Pilsner Urquell loses some of its sparkling hoppy freshness when it is transported any distance. But its soft, malty finish is still evident, as is its dark golden color—and it is still better than any of its rivals.

St. Stan's Red Sky Ale

Brewery: Stanislaus Brewing Company

Address: 821 L Street
Modesto
California 95354
USA

Telephone: 209 524 2337

This microbrewery specializes in altbiers—those beers which are made using top-fermenting yeast, but which are then stored in cellars at cold temperatures before packaging, a technique used in the production of lager.

St. Stan's origins go back to 1973 when Garith Helm and his wife Remy started brewing German-style beers as a hobby, following their "conversion" to the taste after a family holiday. They did this so well and in such quantity that in 1981 they had to build a brewery, on a cattle and horse farm in Modesto, in Stanislaus County, California in Central Valley where the climate is buring hot. Further success led to the building of a larger brewery, in downtown Modesto; it opened in Septrember 1991. It produces 12,000 barrels a year, which can be drunk on the premises—the largest brewpub in California.

St. Stan's is the largest producer of altbiers in the United States; they come in three different style—Amber, Dark, and "Fest." Its latest produce is Red Sky Ale, a top-fermented, cold-conditioned ale, which is quite strong (5.9% by volume), darkish brown, with a distinct bitter taste of hops.

Hürlimann's Samichlaus

Brewery: Brauerei Hürlimann AG

Address: PO Box 654
8027 Zurich
Switzerland

Telephone: 01 288 2626

For many years Hürlimann's Samichlaus (the name means Santa Claus) was recognized as the world's strongest beer at 14% AbV. It is brewed using pure yeast strains and bottom fermentation, and lagered for a year.

Founded in 1836 by Albert Hürlimann, the company became a leader in developing the yeast strains necessary for bottom fermentation and other types of beer, eventually producing a strain of yeast that could ferment beer to a high alcohol level. In 1979 this was used to brew a strong Christmas beer that became popular enough to sustain production each year. It is reddish-brown in color, a blend of light and dark malts, with three types of hops. The yeast is made to work hard and the beer is regularly transferred from vessel to vessel to keep it going. Hallertauer, Hersbrücker, and Styrian hops are used.

Samichlaus avoids the cloying sweetness of other superstrong lagers through long maturation: it is brewed each year—the bottle says that this takes place on Samichlaus Day (6 December, the feast of St Nicholas)—but not released until the same time the following year when it is served in a brandy glass for slow consumption—Drink it with caution!

Samuel Adams Boston Lager

Brewery: The Boston Beer Company

Address: The Brewery
30 Germania Street
Boston
Massachusetts 02130
USA

Telephone: 617 368 5000

The Boston Beer Company epitomizes the changes in brewing that have taken place in the United States in the last fifteen years. Widely available, the company's splendid brews have been excellently marketed—as you would expect from Boston Beer Company founder Jim Koch.

Koch comes from a long line of brewers—five generations, which seemed to be ending in 1956, when Jim's father finished working. But it was in the German-American's blood and after business school young Koch started brewing. The first beer, in 1985, was Boston lager, which was produced at Pittsburg. From 1988, the company has been operating out of the Boston Haffenreffer brewery, originally opened in 1865 and closed a century later.

The company's main products are Samuel Adams Boston Ale, the bottled version of which is made under contract at F. X. Matt, and Boston Lager—bronze-gold-colored, with a soft slightly spicy, malty taste, a flowery aroma and a dry finish. It is hopped three times in the kettle using Fuggles and Saaz hops, and once during maturation with Kent Goldings. The company also does a wheat beer, Samuel Adams Wheat, warmly sweet with slight fruit overtones.

Hallertau
Tettnang
two-row
and pure
American
rich robust
taste. Cheers

SAMUEL ADAMS

SAMUEL ADAMS

BREWER • PATRIOT

BOSTON LAGER

4.8% vol.   THE BEST BEER IN AMERICA™   330 ml

Schneider Weisse

Brewer: G. Schneider & Son

Address: 1-5 Emil Ott Strasse
8420 Kelheim
Bavaria
Germany

Telephone: 09441 7050

Schneider, whose eponymous founder Georg was granted in 1872 the first wheat beer brewing licence from the Wittelsbachs (the Bavarian royal house), produces wheat beers against which all others are judged. Schneider's original beer was sensationally received and he soon had to open a second brewery in Kelheim: this became the company's main plant after the destruction of the first during World War II.

Wheat beers are made from a blend of barley and wheat malts, the barley essential to the process with its higher number of starches that can be turned to sugar and its filtering husks; wheat by itself would clog the brewing vessels. The wheat malt adds a pale hazy color and a distinctive aroma and flavor. The yeast is top fermenting and used for both first and secondary fermentation. The second fermentation takes place in special warm boxes in the brewery in order to have full control over the final product. The result is a very effervescent wheat beer with a refreshing level of carbonation.

The Schneider brewery still follows the original recipe, using the same yeast culture that was first used by Georg Schneider. Nothing is altered for fear that such a change would effect the final outcome—the famous Schneider Weisse (5.4%), with its distinctive tan color, with hints of vanilla and cloves creating a quenching tartness and long finish. Other notable beers also produced by the company include: Aventinus (8.0%)—a strong wheat bock made with a crystal caramalt from Bamberg—dark, sweet and fruity, with an aroma of spices and a dry finish and Weizen Hell.

Sierra Nevada

Brewery: Sierra Nevada Brewing Company

Address: 1075 East 20th Street
Chico
California 95928
USA

Telephone: 916 893 3520

One of the first—and quite possibly the best—of a new generation of craft microbreweries that have sprung up in North America since the 1980s, the Sierra Nevada Brewing Company was started by Ken Grossman and Paul Camusi in 1981. Since then the company has become justifiably famous for its beers.

The company's Sierra Nevada Draught Ale is sweeter in taste than the excellent Pale Ale, which is perfectly poised between the hoppy dryness and the fruity tang of the top fermenting yeast. Sierra Nevada also makes an excellent firm dry porter and a strong stout (6.0% AbV), which is very smooth. There's a holiday winter warmer as well—Celebration Ale—to a different specification each year.

Perhaps the best known beer among aficionados is one of the strongest beers in the USA and a world classic—Big Foot Barley Wine (12.5% AbV). Made with a dark malt and Nugget, Cascade, and Centennial hops, it is matured for four weeks before leaving the brewery. It has a very hoppy and earthy aroma and a strong fruity and spicy alcoholic taste.

PALE ALE

...is a handmade natural ale. There are no additives, or...
...malts, whole hops, brewer's yeast and crystal clear...
...the layer of yeast in each bottle is a result of the Kraeusen...
...which produces carbonation naturally in the...

Purest Ingredients

Finest Quality

SIERRA NEVADA®

CA REDEMPTION VALUE ALC 5.6% BY VOL.

GOVERNMENT WARNING: (1) ACCORDING TO THE SURGEON GENERAL

PALE ALE

NET CONTENTS 12 FL. OZ.

© 1989 S.N.BR. CO.

BREWED & BOTTLED BY SIERRA NEVADA BREWING CO., CHICO, CA

Sol

Brewery: Cervecaria Moctezuma

Address: 156 Lago Alberto
Mexico City 11320
Mexico

Telephone: 05 670 4243

Today's biggest exporter of all the Mexican breweries was also one of the smallest, until its merger with the Cuauhtemoc group. Its main product—along with Modelo's Corona—took the world by storm as 1980s' marketing saw Mexican beer, drunk from transparent bottles with a chunk of lime accompanying, become the byword in cool all around the western world.

This was certainly a case of chic being more important than taste, and because of this connoisseurs have tended to shy away from what is really a very palatable lager. It is unpretentious and thirst-quenching, and at 4.5% AbV is light enough to go with any food.

Sol, which means "Sun" in Spanish, has a tradition that began more than 100 years ago; only some years after its launching, Sol received a Gold Medal in the Universal Exhibition in Paris, France. Since then it has captivated the Mexican and International market with the lightness of its flavor. It has a sparkling gold hue and exciting aroma and flavor of malt. Sol is a refreshingly subtle beer and because of its unequalled attributes, this brand has won a place of preference amongst consumers in many nations.

Cuauhtemoc also brews Dos Equis (see page 36), an excellent Vienna-style lager,. and Bohemia, more like a Pilsener.

IMPORTED BEER

Sol

CERVEZA III

DESDE 1899

BIER BIRRA BIERE

PRODUCT OF MEXICO
BREWED AND BOTTLED BY:
CERVECERIA CUAUHTEMOC MOCTEZUMA.
S.A. DE C.V.   ORIZABA, VER.

33 cl.℮   4.5% alc/vol.

Rep. S.S.A. No. 61555 "B" HECHO EN MEXICO MARCA REGISTRADA

Staropramen

Brewery: Prazske Pivovary (Prague Breweries)

Address: Nadrazni 84, 105 54
Prague 5-Smichov
Czech Republic

Telephone: 02 5719 1111

Prague is every bit as much a great drinking center as Munich, and the locals are justly proud of their breweries, of which Prazske Pivovary is just one of many. Staropramen actually means "old spring" in Czech, and this water is an essential ingredient in the brews, giving it much of its character.

The Staropramen brewery began producing its renowned light and dark lagers in Prague in 1869, though it has now merged with two other Prague breweries, Branik and Mestan. More recently the British Brewing group Bass has also invested heavily in Prague Breweries, and has been heavily instrumental in encouraging the continued use of the traditional brewing technology of horizontal lagering. By keeping this procedure of secondary fermentation, less of the malt sugars turn to alcohol, with a corresponding increase in maltiness to balance the flavor of the hops and give a wonderfully well-rounded full-bodied flavor. Furthermore Bass is exporting the soft and malty Staropramen to the world.

The light or blonde version of Staropramen is 5.0% AbV, contains all this rich fullness with a crisp clean aroma. The dark variant is 4.5% AbV and has a deep ruby-brown color, with a smooth silky palate and a full rich finish.

Steiner Märzen

Brewery: Schlossbrauerei Stein

Address: Schlosshof 2
83371 Stein a.d Traun

Telephone: 08621 38320

Dating back to 1489 the Schlossbrauerei (Castle Brewery) is one of the hidden gems of the brewing scene. The brewery uses old natural caves that have been expanded by hand when the capacity was increased. These natural stone cellars guarantee the constant cool temperatures required for storing bottom-fermented beers.

In addition to Export Hell (the biggest seller), Pils, Weissbier, and Ur-Dunkel, the Schlossbrauerei Stein produces one of the few remaining classic Märzen beers. The brewery uses 100% roasted malts, decoction mash, cold fermentation, and long, cold lagering. The Märzen has a wonderfully complex fruity, malty flavor and aroma and contains 5.5% AbV.

According to tradition, Steiner Märzen is brewed in March and served throughout the summer at local festivals, where it is only available unfiltered and in one-litre mugs.

The other classic produced by the brewery is the complex, toffeeish, nutty Dunkel. It has a deep garnet-red color derived from using 100% dark roasted malts. Both beers are very highly rated in their styles.

Stella Artois Dry

Brewery: NV Interbrew SA

Address: Vaarstraat 94
3000 Leuven
Belgium

Telephone: 016 24 7111

The giant Interbrew group is one of the big boys of world brewing and came about through a merger between Stella Artois of Leuven and Piedboeuf of Jupille-sur-Meuse. Stella traces its origins to the Den Horen tavern that began brewing in 1366. By 1717 it had been bought by one of its recently graduated master-brewers—Sebastien Artois, whose descendants expanded the business, taking over other Leuven breweries and becoming one of Europe's biggest brewing concerns. They switched to the new lagering methods in the late nineteenth century, making a golden, bottom-fermented beer called a Bock. But the company really took off when it introduced its strong Pilsner-type beer—Stella Artois—in 1926.

It is made according to traditional methods, with the malts prepared on floors rather than in tanks before being brewed with Czech Saaz hops which give the finished product a rather spicy aromatic flavor, followed by lagering for approximately two months.

First brewed as a Christmas beer (hence the name Stella—Star), it soon became so popular it was brewed all year round. Clever advertising and marketing has made it hugely exportable and brewed under lincence in several countries. The other leg of Interbrew produces the market-leading Jupiler (5.0 AbV), launched in 1966; Interbrew also produces Lamot Pils.

Tsingtao

Brewery: Tsingtao Brewery

Address: 56 Dengzhou Road
Tsingtao
Shandong 266021
China

China is the second largest brewing country in the world, although until the last century its alcoholic drinks were based on the east's staple produce—rice—rather than grain. It was the opening up of China to Western influences during the nineteenth century that saw the change and the Tsingtao brewery was set up on the Shandong peninsula with the help of German technology.

The investment proved a success and today Tsingtao is the number one consumer-branded product exported from China. First introduced to the United States in 1972, Tsingtao is the main Chinese beer in the United States and is sold in more than 30 countries worldwide, accounting for 90% of China's total beer exports.

Tsingtao is a pale Pilsner style lager (5.2% AbV), with both malt and hops in its aroma and taste, and a dry finish. It goes well with chinese food—and so has benefited from the post-World War 2 growth of quality Chinese restaurants in Europe and around the world. Tsingtao is produced with spring water from Laoshan, a mountain area famous throughout China for the purity of its water. The domestically-grown hops used to brew Tsingtao are of such high quality that they are also exported to European breweries. Tsingtao also uses the finest yeast and barley imported from Australia and Canada in its brewing process.

Tusker

Brewery: Kenya Brewery

Address: Thika Road
Ruaraka
Nairobi
Kenya

The high altitude around the Equator in Kenya makes the growing of hops and barley easy and brewing straightforward, a fact that the British colonists were quick to discover in the 1930s. Determined to create as many home comforts as possible, they had brewing equipment and an experienced brewer sent over from Burtonwood, England. Consequently they set up East African Breweries (which was later to become Kenya Breweries), to cater for the intense local thirst for beer.

Tusker Premium (4.8% AbV), is brewed from 90% pale barley malt grown in Kenya, and 10% local-grown cane sugar, but uses imported Styrian and Hallertauer hops. This combination produces an aromatic and delicate Pilsner-type lager with malty overtones and a mild, dry hoppy finish that has begun to be noticed outside the African continent. This beer was first brought to international notice by Ernest Hemingway—the novelist and notable drinker—who popularized Tusker Premium and White Cap (another Kenya Breweries line) after visiting East Africa on his frequent big game hunts. A premier version of Tusker is used for export —especially to the United States. To remind you of its provenance, the label on the bottle features African wildlife.

TUSKER

BIA NI BORA

12 FL OZ   355 ml

PREMIUM LAGER

Brewed from Bima Equatorial Barley and
the pure waters of Mzinga Murangi

PRODUCT OF KENYA E. AFRICA

Westmalle Tripel

Brewery: Abdij der Trappisten van Westmalle VZW

Address: Antwerpsesteenweg 496
2390 Westmalle
Belgium

Telephone: 03 312 9222

Produced at the monastery of Westmalle—one of only six Trappist establishments brewing in the world, the others being Chimay (see page 30), Orval, Rochefort, Westvleteren, and Schaapskooi—this is a splendid example of pale Triple-style Trappist beer, so beloved of the Belgians and Dutch—but distinct from Abbey beers which are of high quality but brewed by commercial brewers.

Established just outside Antwerp in 1821, Westmalle maintains its monastic sense of withdrawal. Inside, the monks produce three types of beer, a single, known as Extra, kept for the monks themselves, a delicate top-fermented brew; the Double, dark brown and malty, with a dry finish; and the famous Triple, a strong top-fermented pale beer with a full round body and a faint fruity aroma. Its mash hails from German and French Pilsner malts, with a mixed yeast, three separate hopping stages and extra sugar added in the traditional way. It also undergoes a secondary fermentation of one to three months. All this produces a powerful 9.0% AbV, which may have the pale color of a Pils but has the rich taste and the hoppy tang of an ale.

Westmalle

Bier
Tripel

Trappist

Bière
Tripel

Gebrouwen in de Abdij
Trappisten, B 2390 Malle
Bier hergist in de fles
Refermentée en bouteille
Nachgärung in der Flasche
Stat p 0.5HFL-Consigne 0.7FF

5 412343 201337

℮ 33 cl

Alc. 9% Vol.

07.08.99

vóór bij voorkeur
baar inc. meilteerd
haltbar bis & consom
mer de préférence avant

Wychwood Hobgoblin

Brewery: Wychwood Brewery Ltd

Address: The Eagle Maltings
The Croftts
Witney
Oxfordshire
OX8 7AZ
England

Telephone: 01993 702574

Available since December 1995, Wychwood Brewery's Hobgoblin (AbV 5.5%) is described by the brewers as "a powerful, full-bodied, copper-red, well balanced brew, with a moderate hoppy, bitterness." It is splendidly packaged and marketed and shows how small independents can gain international sales.

The Wychwood Brewery is based in the Cotswolds, at Witney in Oxfordshire and uses traditional methods—English malt, hops, yeast, and water from the local Windrush river—to produce its range of ales which includes the interestingly ebullient "Dog's Bollocks," Old Devil, Black Wych Stout, Fiddler's Elbow and Wychwood Special.

The brewery takes its name from the ancient Wychwood forest that surrounded Witney in medieval times. Clinch and Co. had started the Eagle Brewery on the site in 1839 but beer was not brewed there following Courage's 1962 takeover. In 1983 Paddy Glenny started to brew there again and since then expansion has been substantial, thanks in part to Government legislation allowing pubs belonging to big breweries to guest ales. Starting out as just a two-man operation producing 10 barrels a week, Wychwood now produces 200 barrels a week and can now be enjoyed throughout Europe, North America, and Canada.

Further Reading

Baillie, Frank; *The Beer Drinker's Companion*; David & Charles, 1973

Beaumont, Stephen; *A Taste for Beer*; Storey Communications, Inc, 1995

Delos, Gilbert; *Beers of the World*; Tiger Books, 1994.

Dunkling, Leslie; *The Guinness Drinking Companion*; Guinness Publishing Ltd, 1992.

Jackson, Michael; *Pocket Beer Book*; Mitchell Beazley, 1995.

Jackson, Michael; *Beer Companion* (Second Edition); Mitchell Beazley, 1997.

Madgin, Hugh; *Best of British Bottled Beer*; Dial House, 1995

Pepper, Barry; *The International Book of Beer*; Todtri, 1996.

Protz, Roger; *Classic Bottled Beers of the World*; Prion, 1997.

Protz, Roger; *Classic Stout & Porter of the World*; Prion, 1997

Protz, Roger; *The Ultimate Encyclopedia of Beer*; Carlton, 1995.

Rolling Rock is brewed in Latrobe, near Pittsburgh, PA.